DATE DUE			

11FL01821

660.6
MOR

Morgan, Sally.

Body doubles :
cloning plants and
animals

BODY DOUBLES
CLONING PLANTS AND ANIMALS
REVISED AND UPDATED

SALLY MORGAN

science at the edge

Heinemann Library
Chicago, Illinois

© 2009 Heinemann Library
an imprint of Capstone Global Library, LLC
Chicago, Illinois

Customer service 888-454-2279

Visit our website at www.heinemannraintree.com

Printed and bound in China by South China Printing Company Ltd.

13 12 11 10 09
10 9 8 7 6 5 4 3 2 1

New edition ISBN: 978 1 4329 2454 6 (hardcover)

The Library of Congress has cataloged the first edition as follows:
Morgan, Sally.
    Body doubles : cloning / Sally Morgan.
        p. cm.
Includes bibliographical references and index.
    ISBN 1-58810-698-5 (HC), 1-4034-4120-0 (Pbk.)
I. Cloning--Juvenile literature. [I. Cloning.] I. Title.
QH442.2 .M67 2002
660.6'5--dc21
                                2001006078

Acknowledgments
The author and publishers are grateful to the following for permission to reproduce copyright material:
© Corbis pp. **27** (Reuters), **57** (Jason Horowitz/Zefa); FLPA/Holt p. **34**; © Imagestate p. **40**; © Kobal p. **8**; © Photolibrary Group/OSF pp. **48**, **50**, **52**; © Photoshot/NHPA p. **12**; © Science Photo Library pp. **4**, **17** (Philippe Plailly/Eurelios), **7** (John Mitchell), **9**, **21** (James King-Holmes), **10** (A.B. Dowsett), **15**, **33** (Klaus Guldbrandsen), **20** (Biophoto Associates), **28** (Peter Menzel), **30** (CNRI), **32** (J.C. Revy), **36** (Juergen Berger), **39** (Professors P.M. Motta & S. Makabe), **42** (L. Willatt, East Anglian Regional Genetics Service), **45** (Dr Yorgos Nikas), **54** (Steve Woit/AgstockUSA); © The Garden Collection p. **13** (Liz Eddison).

Cover photograph of cloned cows reproduced with permission of © Corbis/Jim Richardson.

CONTENTS

Some words are printed in bold, like this. You can find out what they mean by looking in the glossary.

INTRODUCTION

On July 5, 1996, Dolly was born. Dolly is probably the most famous sheep in the world. The reason for her fame was that she was a clone. She was genetically identical to her mother, a sheep that was born six years earlier. Dolly had exactly the same **genes** as her mother. This was a major achievement in the field of **genetics**, the biological equivalent to splitting the atom or breaking the sound barrier. Before Dolly's birth, many scientists thought it was impossible to clone an adult cell. Since her birth, the potential development of cloning technology has both excited and worried people.

Dolly was the first clone of an adult cell to be produced. She was a perfectly normal sheep and gave birth to healthy lambs. However, she suffered from arthritis and died from lung disease at the relatively young age of six.

What Is Cloning?

Cloning is creating a genetically identical copy of an individual. Cloning itself is not new. Identical human twins are natural clones. Just after **fertilization**, the newly formed cell splits into two identical halves, and each half continues to develop normally. The result is two identical people—clones. Children of the same parents usually look different. They are similar in that half their genes come from their father and half from their mother. However, the actual mix of genes in each case is different. Identical twins also have genes from each parent, but their genes are the same. Gardeners produce clones of plants by taking cuttings (pieces from the original parent plant), which develop into plants that are identical to the parent plants. This is called vegetative propagation, but it is the same principle as cloning.

DISCUSS   Cloning Concerns

Scientists and many other people believe that, if carefully regulated, cloning could be used to benefit people. For example, cloning offers hope to many people suffering from diseases such as **Parkinson's** disease and **leukemia**. Many people with leukemia need a **bone marrow transplant**. They may be lucky and have a close relative with compatible cells. Otherwise they have to hope somebody on a bone marrow register (a list of potential donors) has cells that will work for them. The chance of finding a match for bone marrow cells is less than one in 20,000, and some people die waiting. Cloning could change that. Doctors could use cloning techniques to produce bone marrow cells identical to those of the patient.

The issue of human cloning is one that concerns many people. Some fear the consequences that would occur if doctors or scientists were able to produce human clones, including the possibility of health defects. In addition, many people have **ethical** and religious objections. Should ethical views overrule scientific research if the outcome may be lifesaving? Or is cloning itself far too risky?

In this book you will learn about **DNA** and **chromosomes**, the difference between cloning plants and animals, how cloning can be used in transplant surgery, and issues associated with cloning human cells. You will also find the answers to questions such as: Is Dolly the only cloned animal? Is it legal to clone humans? And can the dead be cloned?

THE PATH TO DOLLY

The research institute where Dolly the sheep was born in July 1996 kept the news of her birth secret until February 1997. When the news was finally released, it made headlines around the world. In the months that followed, cloning was rarely out of the news. Although there was a great deal of excitement, the news also raised concerns about the possibilities introduced by this major advance in our knowledge of genetics.

People have thought about cloning for thousands of years, long before there was knowledge of genetics or biochemistry. However, it was not until the end of the 19th century that the science of genetics began to develop, when scientists started studying **embryology** using microscopes. One of the most important embryologists of this time was Hans Spemann, a Nobel Prize winner, who published the book *Embryonic Development and Induction* in 1938. From a salamander (a type of amphibian), Spemann took an **embryo** that consisted of just two cells and split it in two. Each of the embryos developed into a normal salamander. They were identical copies, or clones, of each other. In his book, Spemann proposed doing an experiment that would involve removing a **nucleus** from an adult salamander cell and placing it in an egg that had its nucleus removed. It was not until 1952, years after Spemann's death, that this experiment was carried out successfully.

Eggs, Tadpoles, and Toads

During the 1950s, scientists Robert Briggs, Tom King, and (later) John Gurdon experimented using the eggs of frogs and toads. They cloned frogs and toads by removing the nucleus from an egg and replacing it with a nucleus taken from a cell of a tadpole. However, they were unable to successfully clone a cell taken from an adult frog or toad.

These experiments captured the public's imagination. If Dolly had been born at this time, the public reaction would have been different. During the 1950s and 1960s many people thought that these kinds of experiments could be beneficial and were to be encouraged. Few people raised concerns over the risks and ethics of cloning. Today, there is much more public debate, and there are numerous committees that consider ethical issues and advise governments. Such pressure can force governments to change laws to prevent scientists from experimenting with human cloning.

During the 1950s and 1960s, many scientists studied frogs' eggs, including those of the leopard frog. Frogs' eggs are large and easy to manipulate, making them good for research.

Although Hans Spemann was the first to describe the process of cloning, he called it nuclear transplantation. The term *clone* (the Greek word for "twig") was first used by the British biologist J.B.S. Haldane in 1963. He was speaking at a convention about the future of science, speculating on how long people would live in the future, how they would fight disease, and whether the cloning of humans would be possible. The brightest and the best of society, he suggested, could be cloned in order to further human achievement.

"We got a good deal of reaction, both from scientists and nonscientists. They thought it was phenomenal. We thought we could clone any cell."

Tom King, talking about the work he carried out on cloning during the 1950s

A Change in Mood

By the 1970s the mood of the public had changed. The first steps in **genetic engineering** had been made and the world's first test-tube baby was born. This involved the technique of **in vitro fertilization**, in which an egg is taken from a woman, fertilized in the laboratory, and then replaced in the woman's **uterus** to develop into a baby. However, many people became concerned about this process. Geneticists were developing more complex procedures and science fiction writers were publishing books predicting that cloning could have terrible consequences. In 1978 a science writer published a book claiming that a human had been cloned. The book was presented as the "true" story of a secret project to produce a clone of a man who had paid a million dollars to a scientist. The story was finally revealed to be a hoax, but the book was a bestseller. The book raised concerns for scientists and society as a whole. They did not want similar things to happen in real life.

During the 1980s hundreds of experiments in which scientists tried to clone mammals failed. Many leading scientists thought that cloning would be impossible. The breakthrough came in 1986, when sheep and cows were successfully cloned from embryo cells. However, scientists still could not successfully clone an adult cell.

The concept of cloning was featured in many science fiction movies from the 1980s and 1990s. The film *Blade Runner* featured human clones that were created to be drones, or workers, on other planets, but the clones revolted and returned to Earth to destroy their creators. *Jurassic Park* featured dinosaurs that were created by cloning.

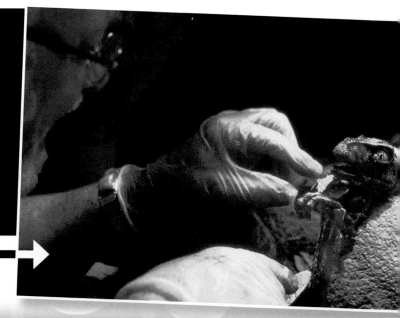

In the science fiction film *Jurassic Park*, scientists reconstructed the DNA of dinosaurs, which enabled them to produce living dinosaurs for a theme park.

Cloning, however, is very real. In 1995 a team led by Ian Wilmut at the Roslin Institute in Scotland successfully cloned two sheep. Their names were Morag and Megan. A year later Dolly was born. She was the first clone to be produced by taking a nucleus from an adult cell and placing it into an empty egg cell. The arrival of Dolly took many people, including scientists, by surprise. For years they had convinced themselves that it was impossible to make a clone of an adult cell.

"I am not a fool. I know what is bothering people about this. I understand why the world is suddenly at my door. But this is my work. It has always been my work and it doesn't have anything to do with creating copies of human beings. I am not haunted by what I do, if that is what you want to know. I sleep very well at night."

Ian Wilmut, speaking about his work in the field of cloning

FOCUS Dolly's Creator: Ian Wilmut

Ian Wilmut was the embryologist who produced Dolly. He worked at the Roslin Institute for 23 years and on the cloning project for 10 years. The careful research he undertook required endless patience. He worked long hours over a microscope, studying embryonic cells. Knowing that many lifesaving drugs were either difficult or expensive to produce, his aim was to create animals that could produce drugs for human use. He wanted to alter their DNA so that they had new genes to give them the ability to make a human drug. However, it was important to be able to produce many of these animals. Once an animal with new abilities had been created, Wilmut needed a technique to clone it—and so his research led to the cloning of adult cells. The creation of Dolly was a huge scientific breakthrough (see pages 24–25).

Morag and Megan were identical twins. They were cloned from the same embryo that was just a few days old. The method by which they were produced was different from the one that produced Dolly.

NATURAL CLONING

This book is concerned with cloning that is carried out artificially in a laboratory. However, cloning is a process that occurs naturally, too. Cloning is used by many microorganisms, or single-celled animals, and plants in order to reproduce and increase in number.

Many organisms reproduce asexually, such as bacteria, amoebas (single-celled organisms that live in water), yeast, and hydras (related to the sea anemone). This means that one individual reproduces on its own without the involvement of another individual. These organisms reproduce asexually when conditions are ideal for an increase in population size, for example, when there is plenty of food and space. All the new individuals are identical to the parent, so they are clones of one another. When conditions change, these organisms reproduce sexually, which involves two individuals.

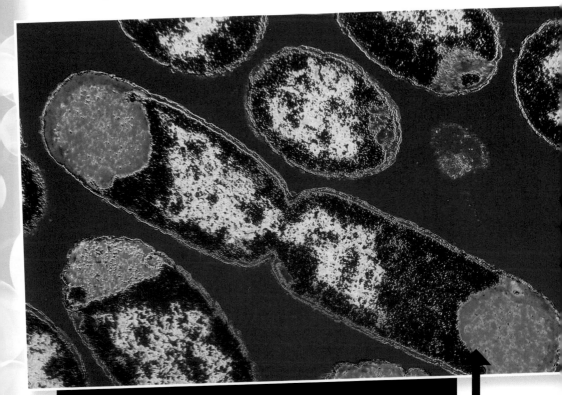

A bacterium undergoes binary fission. The cell simply divides in two. The two new daughter cells are genetically identical to each other.

Binary Fission and Budding

Bacteria and amoebas can divide in two through a process called binary fission. When an amoeba is ready to reproduce, it splits in two; the nucleus divides, then the rest of the cell divides. This produces two small amoebas that feed and grow. Under ideal conditions, an amoeba can divide once a day. Bacteria divide in a similar way, but at a faster rate than amoebas—every 20 minutes in ideal conditions. One bacterium can become a million bacteria in just seven hours!

Hydra and yeast cells reproduce asexually through budding. A hydra reproduces by growing a new hydra out of its side. At first, the new bud gets its food from the parent, until it becomes large enough to break away and live independently. Yeast is a fungus, but unlike many other types of fungi, it consists of single cells. When a yeast cell is large enough, it produces a small outgrowth, or bud, which gradually gets larger. Eventually the bud breaks off to form a new cell.

Spores

Many fungi produce spores asexually. Spores are tiny, round structures that grow into a new individual. One fungus is the pin mold, which grows on bread and other foods. It consists of a mass of tiny threads called hyphae that grow over the surface of the food source, absorbing it. A few hyphae grow vertically, and their ends become swollen. Inside, thousands of tiny spores are produced. They are released into the air and scattered by air currents.

Plant Reproduction

Asexual reproduction also occurs in plants. The strawberry plant produces side-shoots called runners, which grow along the ground. Roots appear at intervals and grow into the soil. The runners between the roots wither away, leaving a row of daughter plants. Shoots called tillers grow from grasses and stolons grow from blackberries. Runners, tillers, and stolons allow plants to increase in number quickly.

Potato plants reproduce asexually by producing tubers. During the summer months, the potato plant makes food using **photosynthesis**. The food moves to underground stems, which swell up and form tubers where the food is stored as starch. By late autumn, the potato shoots above the ground die, but the tubers survive underground. In spring, the food in the tuber is used for new growth. Each tuber begins to grow into a new plant. Because all the new plants come from the same parent, they are clones.

A strawberry plant produces a shoot called a runner, which grows along the ground. New plants form at intervals along this shoot.

Cloning Plants

People have artificially cloned plants for hundreds of years. However, the word *cloning* is not normally used. Instead, gardeners refer to the process as vegetative propagation. One example of this is when cuttings are taken. If you cut a length of shoot off a plant and place it in a glass of water, after a few weeks you will probably see roots appearing at the end of the shoot. Once the cutting has rooted, it can be planted in soil to grow into a new plant.

Gardeners can take cuttings of most plants in order to produce new, identical plants cheaply and quickly. Agricultural companies also use vegetative propagation because it enables large numbers of identical plants to be produced in a short period of time.

New plants can be grown from seed, too. Seeds are produced by **sexual reproduction**. The pollen from one flower is transferred to another flower and the male sex cells in the pollen fertilize the female egg. The resulting seeds have new combinations of genes and are all different. When plants with new features are wanted, the process of sexual reproduction is useful. By crossing selected plants there is a chance that the new combination of genes will produce a plant with a certain desired feature, such as a new color of flower. Once the desired plant has been produced, vegetative propagation is the only way to produce more plants with the same feature. Doing so ensures all offspring are identical to the parent, and the new feature is not lost.

Gardeners produce new plants by taking cuttings. A cutting is a short length of shoot with some of its leaves removed. The cutting is dipped in a rooting powder that stimulates the formation of roots from the bottom of the cutting.

MICROPROPAGATION

The propagation methods used commercially are slightly different from those used by gardeners, since plant companies have to produce large numbers of high-quality plants. One of the methods companies use is called micropropagation, or plant-tissue culture. It uses a single plant to produce a large number of clones. A short length of shoot is taken from the parent plant. This is called an explant. It is sterilized and transferred onto a jellylike **growth medium**, which encourages the growth of shoots. The shoot that grows is divided again into many smaller pieces, each of which is grown on fresh growth medium. Then the shoots are transferred to a different medium that encourages root growth. After about four weeks, the plantlets (young plants) are large enough to be planted into sterile compost.

Micropropagation has a number of advantages:
- It is quick.
- It produces a large number of identical plants from one or a few parent plants.
- It retains all the good features of the parental material, such as color or shape of flower, disease-resistance, or high yield.
- It is cost-effective.
- It is easy to transport many plants under sterile conditions.
- Only healthy plants are produced.
- It eliminates problems with seasonal production because it can be carried out all year round.

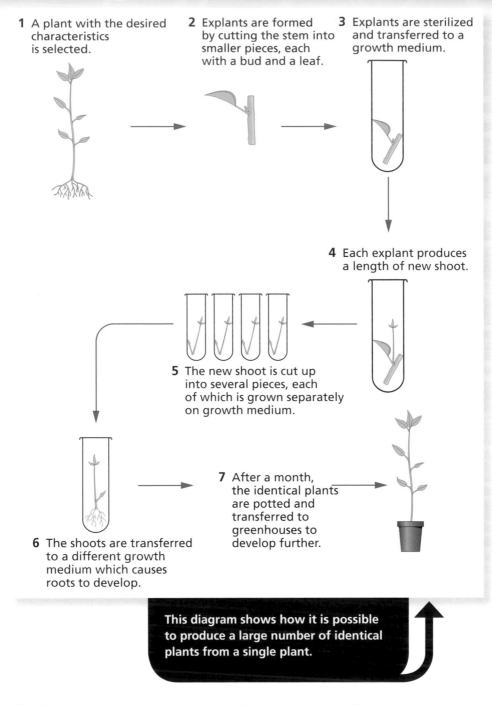

1 A plant with the desired characteristics is selected.

2 Explants are formed by cutting the stem into smaller pieces, each with a bud and a leaf.

3 Explants are sterilized and transferred to a growth medium.

4 Each explant produces a length of new shoot.

5 The new shoot is cut up into several pieces, each of which is grown separately on growth medium.

6 The shoots are transferred to a different growth medium which causes roots to develop.

7 After a month, the identical plants are potted and transferred to greenhouses to develop further.

This diagram shows how it is possible to produce a large number of identical plants from a single plant.

Cloning plants is relatively straightforward. It is possible to clone a whole plant from a single cell. This is because every plant cell, if given the right set of conditions and chemicals, has the ability to produce unspecialized plant cells that can be cultured to produce a whole plant.

PROTOPLAST CLONING

Improved cloning techniques mean that it is now possible to clone a plant from a single cell. A small sample of tissue is removed from a plant and treated with an **enzyme** to remove the **cellulose** cell wall around each plant cell. All that is left is the protoplast, which is a cell without its cell wall. The protoplasts are cultured individually under sterile conditions. First, they grow into a mass of unspecialized cells called a callus. Then the callus is placed on a different growth medium, which causes some of the cells to turn into roots and others to become shoots. This forms a tiny but complete plant.

FOCUS Micropropagation Units

A few botanic gardens have set up micropropagation units to propagate plants that are rare, **endangered**, or difficult to propagate conventionally. The unit at the Royal Botanic Gardens near London, England, has propagated a wide range of plants. Researchers there have become experts in the micropropagation of plants that are rarely, if ever, worked on elsewhere. At any one time, researchers are working on approximately 500 species from all over the world. Many are rare and endangered species found on islands and are particularly at risk. Projects include the propagation of rare plants from St. Helena, the Mascarene Islands, Hawaii, and the Canary Islands. Successful micropropagation often produces more plantlets than are required. The surplus plants are distributed to other botanic gardens around the world. Where conditions allow, some of these plants will be used in attempts to return them to their country of origin. Some examples are rare orchids from Borneo, and a variety of plants from the Canary Islands.

The young plants in these jars have been produced by tissue culture at a micropropagation unit. They are clones of the original plant.

CHROMOSOMES AND DNA

Scientists working in the field of cloning must clearly understand the role of the genes in a cell before they can begin their research into cloning animals.

The body uses a set of instructions known as DNA to work properly. These instructions are found in almost every cell. They tell a cell what substances to make, how to grow, when to divide, and how to repair itself. In fact, they control every process that takes place in a cell. Every organism inherits these instructions from its parents. The instructions take the form of a chemical code that is located on the chromosomes within the nucleus of each cell.

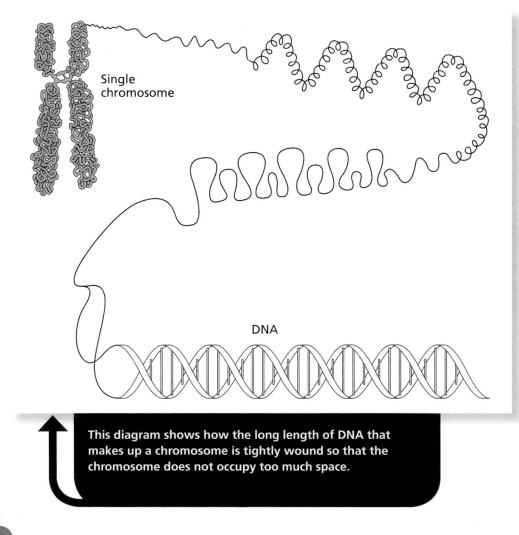

Single chromosome

DNA

This diagram shows how the long length of DNA that makes up a chromosome is tightly wound so that the chromosome does not occupy too much space.

The Makeup of Chromosomes and DNA

A chromosome is a very long, thin strand made of DNA. The number of chromosomes in a cell is unique to each organism. A human cell has 46, a locust cell has 22, and a cabbage cell has only 18. In human cells the 46 chromosomes occur in pairs. Exceptions are red blood cells that have no chromosomes, and human sex cells (the **sperm** and egg). The sex cells are produced by a special kind of cell division in which the chromosome number halves—each contains 23 chromosomes, one from each pair. At fertilization, a sperm fuses with an egg to form a new cell called a **zygote**. The combined number of chromosomes in a zygote is 46. The zygote divides, becomes an embryo, and can grow into a new human.

A chromosome is subdivided into genes. Imagine a chromosome as a string of beads, with each bead representing a gene. A single chromosome can be made up of hundreds of genes. In total, there are about 30,000 different genes carried by the chromosomes in a human body. Genes control the production of **proteins**. Each gene is responsible for the production of a particular protein. So far, scientists only know the job of a few hundred genes, but in the near future, they may know the position and role of every single one.

The DNA **molecule** is made up of two strands that twist around each other to form a double helix. The sides of the chain are made of alternating sugar and phosphate molecules, while the "rungs" link the molecules.

A gene is a specific length of DNA on a chromosome. DNA is a huge, coiled molecule. There are two strands twisted together in a spiral called a helix. It is shaped like a twisted ladder, with sides made from alternating sugar and phosphate molecules. The rungs of the ladder are formed by a link between molecules called bases. There are four different bases: adenine (A), guanine (G), cytosine (C), and thymine (T). The A and G bases are larger than the C and T bases. To make sure that the rungs are always the same width, A only pairs with T, and C only pairs with G.

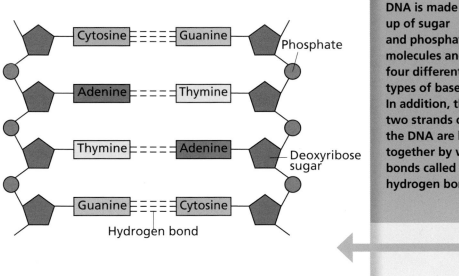

DNA is made up of sugar and phosphate molecules and four different types of bases. In addition, the two strands of the DNA are held together by weak bonds called hydrogen bonds.

Cell Specialization

As well as understanding the role of DNA within a cell, embryologists have to know how cells behave and how they become specialized to do a particular job.

At fertilization, a sperm fuses with an egg cell. The fertilized egg cell (zygote) gains one set of genes from the father and a second set from the mother, so its genetic material is a combination of both parents' genes. The zygote starts to undergo cell division and becomes an embryo, which develops into a new individual. Every cell in the body of this new individual arises from the same fertilized egg and this means that every cell has the same set of genes.

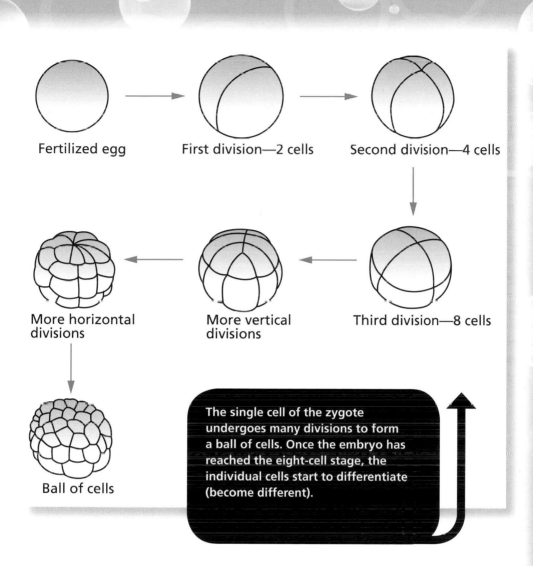

Fertilized egg

First division—2 cells

Second division—4 cells

More horizontal divisions

More vertical divisions

Third division—8 cells

Ball of cells

The single cell of the zygote undergoes many divisions to form a ball of cells. Once the embryo has reached the eight-cell stage, the individual cells start to differentiate (become different).

DIFFERENTIATION

As shown above, the zygote divides into two cells, which each divide to make four cells. Each cell then divides again and again. Soon, there is a hollow ball of cells. At this stage, all cells are the same. After about 14 days, the cells start to take on a different appearance. Their structure changes in order to carry out different jobs, such as nerve cells, skin cells, and liver cells. This process of specialization is called differentiation. Eventually, there will be hundreds of different types of cells, each specialized for a particular job. Once a cell has reached its final form, its appearance will not alter. So although the genes in a liver cell and a nerve cell are the same, the cells look different and have different jobs.

SWITCHING GENES ON AND OFF

The DNA in an unspecialized cell is the same as the DNA in a specialized cell. However, during the process of cell specialization, some of the genes are switched off, while others are left on. The active genes are those that are required for the cell's specialized functions. Any genes that are not required are switched off. Therefore, a nerve cell has a different set of active genes from a liver cell.

A term that is used a lot in genetics is *gene expression*. It refers to a gene being switched on and being able to have an effect or express itself. Many hormones and drugs work by switching on or off particular genes in the body in order to control the production of a certain protein by that gene.

One of the biggest challenges for embryologists is to take a specialized cell, such as a liver cell, and return the cell to an unspecialized condition—with all its genes switched on.

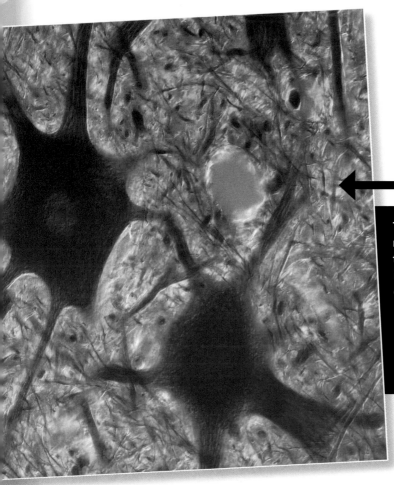

This image shows a mass of nerve cells in the brain. A nerve cell is specialized to carry out the specific job of sending electrical impulses from one nerve cell to another.

The Human Genome Project

One of the most ambitious biological projects ever undertaken began in 1990, with teams of scientists from all around the world taking part. The aim of the Human Genome Project was to discover the sequence of bases that make up all the genes in human DNA, the genome being the complete set of genetic information contained within a cell. This was not an easy task. Our genes make up only five per cent of DNA and are separated by long lengths of non-functional DNA—nicknamed "junk" DNA. In 2001 the first draft of the human **genetic code** was published. This information has yet to be used effectively. It can be compared to a foreign language dictionary. It is almost impossible to generate meaningful sentences just using the human genome dictionary. The next stage is to understand which combination of words—or co-expressed genes—are important to biological processes. Since 2001 other projects have been set up. The ENCODE project aims to analyze specific sequences with a particular function, and the Cancer Genome Atlas hopes to identify genes linked to human cancers.

This researcher is carefully preparing DNA to be used for sequencing for the Human Genome Project.

CLONING IN THE LAB

Cloning plants is relatively simple, but cloning animals, especially mammals, is far more complex. Think about a plant cutting. The new cells that form at the end of the cutting, if given the right nutrients, will develop into root cells. The same is not true of most animals. If a person's arm is cut off, it will not sprout a new body. Once an animal cell has become specialized, it cannot revert to being unspecialized. Scientists working with animal cloning have to figure out how they can transfer the genetic material of a specialized cell into an unspecialized cell and then switch on all of its genes.

Specialized Cells

A human body contains hundreds of different kinds of cells, and there are billions of each kind. A liver cell has one set of active genes, while a muscle cell has another. This is what makes the cells different. In the previous chapter you read about how the cells become specialized (see pages 19 and 20). The critical stage in differentiation is when the embryo becomes a ball of eight cells. It is at this stage that the process of change begins, a change that cannot be reversed.

Embryologists have discovered that any cell removed from the embryo up to the eight-cell stage can survive on its own and continue to divide to form a new, but identical, individual. It has all the genetic information needed to produce the whole range of cell types. The same process occurs when identical twins are produced. In fact, embryologists have produced identical quintuplet sheep from five of the eight cells of an eight-cell sheep embryo. The technique is relatively simple. The cells are carefully pulled apart, allowed to grow, and then placed in the uterus of a **surrogate** mother sheep. After the eight-cell stage, the cells lose their ability to produce all the different tissues that make up a complete organism.

Methods of Cloning

There are two main methods of animal cloning: embryo cloning and **nuclear transfer**. So far, most animal clones have been produced using embryo cloning. In this method, the embryos produced are not identical to either parent because there is a mix of genes from both parents.

Embryo Cloning

The method of cloning a cow using the technique of embryo cloning is as follows:

1. A sample of sperm is taken from a bull with the desired features.
2. The sample is placed in a glass petri dish that contains an egg taken from a cow.
3. In vitro fertilization occurs.
4. The single fertilized cell divides to form two cells, which divide to form four cells, and then again to form a ball of eight cells.
5. The tiny embryo is carefully split to form more embryos. Each of these embryos is identical—they are clones of one another. However, unlike in plant cloning, the embryos are not identical to either parent as there is a mix of genes from both parents.
6. Each embryo is transferred into the uterus of a cow—the surrogate mother.

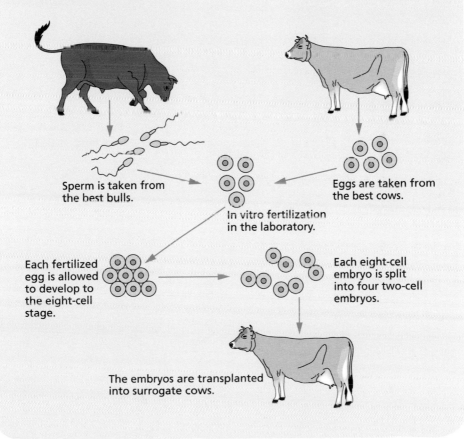

Sperm is taken from the best bulls.

Eggs are taken from the best cows.

In vitro fertilization in the laboratory.

Each fertilized egg is allowed to develop to the eight-cell stage.

Each eight-cell embryo is split into four two-cell embryos.

The embryos are transplanted into surrogate cows.

CLONING BY NUCLEAR TRANSFER

The nuclear transfer method, which was used to create Dolly, is different from embryo cloning because it produces a clone identical to the parent. This method can be used to recreate animals with useful characteristics, such as cows with a high milk yield (see page 29). Cloning the animals retains their desirable features. Its genes are not mixed with genes from another parent and diluted.

DISCUSS Poor Success Rates and Other Concerns

Cloning does not have a very high success rate. The creation of Dolly sounds simple, but was actually incredibly difficult and there were many failures. The process of fusing the udder cell with an egg cell was tried 277 times. Only 29 embryos were obtained, which were grown for a week and then placed in different surrogate sheep. After all that, only one lamb, Dolly, was born.

Many cloned animals are not born healthy. They may be unusually large and many do not live long. It is possible that tiny changes made to the genes affect the production of proteins essential to the animal's survival. One day, scientists may be able to screen cloned embryos for a higher success rate.

Concerns that a newly born clone would have DNA that was as old as the parent cell have also been raised. For example, Dolly was born with the same DNA as her mother, a six-year-old ewe. Nobody is sure what effect this could have. Some scientists have commented on the fact that cloned animals have parts missing from the ends of their chromosomes, which could shorten their life span. In Dolly's case, by the time she was five-and-a-half years old, she had developed arthritis. This painful condition causes joints to become swollen and usually only develops in older animals. Dolly then developed a lung disease. Due to the extent of her illness, scientists knew that Dolly would not recover. They decided to euthanize her (humanely kill her with an injection). Scientists studying her remains hope they will be able to tell if her health problems were related to cloning.

The low success and high mortality rates have convinced many people that cloning is not ethical. As a result, animal rights activists believe this research should be banned. What do you think? It is worth considering that problems may only be solved with continued research.

"There have been reports of high mortality in cloned cows and sheep. Clones have died hours or days after delivery or had abnormally high birth weights."

Philip Damiani, research scientist, Advanced Cell Technology

How Was Dolly Created?

Dolly's mother was a six-year-old Finn Dorset ewe. Cells were taken from her udder and grown for a week in a low-nutrient growth medium. This medium kept the cells alive, but stopped them from dividing. An unfertilized egg was then removed from a Scottish Blackface ewe. The nucleus, containing the DNA, was sucked out. One of the **donor** sheep's udder cells was slipped under the outer membrane of the egg. A tiny burst of electricity was passed through them, causing the donor cell to fuse with the egg cell. Now the egg cell had a new nucleus—the nucleus of the udder cell. A second burst of electricity jump-started the cell into dividing. Soon, there was a ball of cells. This was allowed to grow for a week before being transferred into the uterus of another Scottish Blackface ewe. The embryo continued to develop, and 148 days later, Dolly was born! Although Dolly was born to a Scottish Blackface ewe, she was identical to her real mother, the Finn Dorset ewe.

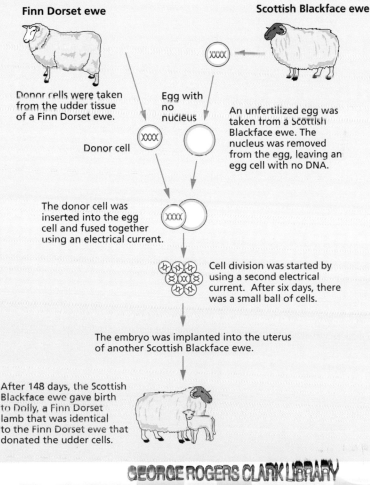

Finn Dorset ewe

Scottish Blackface ewe

Donor cells were taken from the udder tissue of a Finn Dorset ewe.

Donor cell

Egg with no nucleus

An unfertilized egg was taken from a Scottish Blackface ewe. The nucleus was removed from the egg, leaving an egg cell with no DNA.

The donor cell was inserted into the egg cell and fused together using an electrical current.

Cell division was started by using a second electrical current. After six days, there was a small ball of cells.

The embryo was implanted into the uterus of another Scottish Blackface ewe.

After 148 days, the Scottish Blackface ewe gave birth to Dolly, a Finn Dorset lamb that was identical to the Finn Dorset ewe that donated the udder cells.

CLONING IN ACTION

Although the techniques of cloning are far from perfect, enough is known for scientists to make use of them in other research projects. Cloning will allow scientists to manufacture drugs in new ways and improve livestock, such as chickens, sheep, and cows.

A Living Drugs Factory

Many drugs are difficult and expensive to make. A single dose can cost hundreds of dollars. This means that their use has to be limited. Genetic engineering and cloning offer a way to change the genetic makeup of an animal so that it can make a drug. For example, a cow or a sheep can be genetically engineered so that the female produces a particular drug, usually in the form of a protein, in her milk. The protein is then extracted from the milk. Proteins can be difficult to create in a laboratory. Using animals to produce proteins is an effective way of manufacturing large quantities of a pure product.

FOCUS — Megan, Morag, and Polly: Proteins in Genetically Engineered Sheep

The first animal genetically engineered for drug manufacture was a sheep that made the human protein alpha-1 antitrypsin, used to treat an inherited lung disease. The method that produced the protein was very unpredictable. Scientists removed the gene responsible for making the protein from human DNA and injected it into sheep embryos. They did this to thousands of embryos in the hope that a few would take up the gene and be able to make the protein. Megan and Morag were the first sheep born (see page 9) in this process. Genetically engineered sheep are not allowed to reproduce, as the ability to produce the protein may be lost. If more sheep are required, scientists either have to repeat the method of inserting the gene into embryos or find a way of cloning the engineered sheep. In fact, research behind the creation of Dolly was aimed at finding a way of cloning genetically engineered sheep such as Megan and Morag. There is now another cloned sheep, Polly, at the Roslin Institute. She has had a human gene inserted into her DNA so that she produces milk containing human factor IX. This blood-clotting agent is needed by people with the disease hemophilia B.

BIOFACTORIES

Like sheep, chickens have been genetically altered. Researchers at the Roslin Institute have produced chickens that lay eggs containing an **antibody**, which can be used to treat malignant melanomas, a type of skin cancer. Extracting the drug from the white of an egg is a simple process. It is much cheaper to have a flock of genetically altered hens, each laying 300 eggs a year, than it is to build a new factory to produce the drug. The next step is to increase the amount of the drug produced in each egg.

"Once you've got the gene in you can breed up hundreds of birds from one cockerel—because they can be bred with hundreds of hens—and you can collect an egg a day and have hundreds of chicks in no time."

Dr. Helen Sang, Roslin Institute, Scotland, on genetically altered chickens

A scientist at the Roslin Institute uses a light to examine the development of cells inside an egg. The scientists—who also created Dolly—have made an agreement with a U.S. biotech company to breed chickens that produce lifesaving drugs in their eggs.

Cloned Farm Animals

Cloning offers a way for farmers to improve their stock over a short period of time. Currently, most farmers use the lengthy process of selective breeding to improve their stock. They choose animals with desirable characteristics to be parents of the new generation of animals. They use **artificial insemination** to help them. **Semen** is taken from male animals that show desirable characteristics. It is frozen and stored for future use. Farmers can purchase the semen and use it to fertilize their animals. However, this process is not reliable and it may take several generations before the desirable characteristics are produced.

Farmers regularly use the method of artificial insemination to fertilize cows. They use semen taken from a bull that has desirable characteristics. Semen from the best bulls may be used to fertilize hundreds of cows around the world.

Cows only produce one calf at a time, but some farmers are using embryo cloning to produce a larger number of calves. The parents are carefully chosen and the embryo they produce is split to produce many identical copies. Each of the clones is placed into a surrogate mother. Although more calves are produced, none is identical to a single parent. Greater improvements might be made once cloning by nuclear transfer becomes more common. In the future, farmers may be able to buy embryos that are clones of the most productive cows from the best herds. This method has the potential to lift the quality of a farmer's herd within one or two generations.

It is likely that specialist companies could sell cloned embryos in much the same way as they now sell semen. Farmers would choose cloned embryos from a catalog that includes descriptions of different animals' traits, such as fertility (the ability to produce offspring), health, and long-term performance. The cloned embryo would then be delivered to the farm for implanting into one of the farmer's own cows.

"The moral issues raised by cloning are neither large nor more profound than the questions human beings have already faced in regard to such technologies as nuclear energy, recombinant DNA, and computer encryption. They are simply new."

From an open letter written by the International Academy of Humanists in 1997. The signatories include Francis Crick (who, with James Watson, discovered the structure of DNA) and Richard Dawkins (Professor of the Public Understanding of Science at Oxford University and author of the book *The Selfish Gene*).

DISCUSS Is Cloning Beneficial?

In 1997 a dairy cow named Zita was the highest-ranked Holstein cow in the United States. She produced almost 18,000 liters (4,755 gallons) of milk, with 5.1 percent butterfat, almost double the national average. Her daughters and granddaughters were just as productive. Zita was an ideal cow to clone, so tissue samples were taken and stored for future use. In March 2001 cloned calves of Zita were born. They were called Cyagra-Z and Genesis-Z and it was hoped they would be just as productive as the original Zita. Genesis-Z takes after Zita in many ways, but she is not as productive. Cyagra-Z was much smaller than Zita and was a sickly animal. She died in 2007. This case shows just how unreliable the outcomes of cloning can be. Do you think that all the money and time spent on cloning is worth it if it does not always produce the desired result?

SPARE-PART SURGERY

One of the most exciting developments in cloning is in the field of medical research. It is already possible to grow skin cells to repair burned skin in a laboratory. Cloning may also allow doctors to produce a never-ending supply of organs for transplant operations.

Cloning for Medical Treatments

Bone marrow is a liquidlike tissue found in the center of the body's largest bones. It is where red blood cells (which carry oxygen around the body), some white blood cells (involved in the defense against disease), and platelets (which help the blood to clot) form. Because bone marrow has no fixed shape or form, it is considered to be the easiest tissue to clone.

In patients who contract leukemia, the white blood cells multiply out of control. One of the best chances of beating this type of cancer is for the patient to have his or her own bone marrow destroyed and replaced with healthy bone marrow from a donor. It is difficult to find a donor with bone marrow that has the right blood type to match that of the patient. If the bone marrow does not match, the body rejects it. Many people die before a suitable donor can be found.

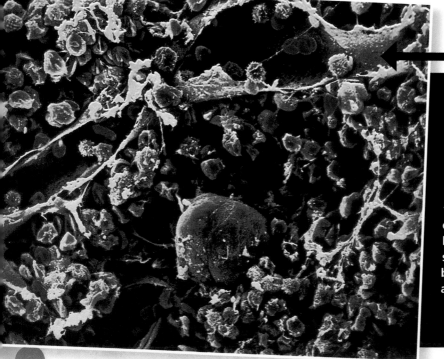

The bone marrow is one of the most important tissues in the body, since it is the site of the formation of new red blood cells, some white blood cells, and platelets.

Cloning could change this. The treatment would involve taking a patient's cell and fusing it with an egg cell that has had its nucleus removed. The egg, with new genes, would start to divide. The critical step would be the addition of chemicals that instruct the cells to become bone marrow cells. If successful, this technique could produce bone marrow cells identical to the patient's own bone marrow and there would be no chance of rejection.

FOCUS Treating Bone Marrow Cancer

Patients with bone marrow cancer often need large doses of antitumor drugs (a tumor is an abnormal growth of cells). Unfortunately, these drugs often kill off healthy bone marrow cells as well as the diseased ones. A possible new treatment involves the removal of the healthy cells, which are then grown in a laboratory and genetically engineered. This involves introducing a gene that gives the healthy cells resistance to the antitumor drug. The engineered cells are injected back into the patient's bone marrow, where they multiply. Then the patient is given the drug. The healthy bone marrow cells are resistant to the drugs, which means that large doses of the drug can be given to kill off the cancer cells. This treatment could increase the patient's chances of survival and making a full recovery.

Artificial Skin

Artificial skin can now be produced from cloned cells to treat burn patients. Skin that has been badly burned needs to be covered to keep it clean, prevent infection, and minimize scarring. Sometimes, if the skin is too badly damaged to repair itself, a skin graft is needed. This involves removing healthy skin from another part of the body and attaching it to the damaged area. Skin is also available from tissue banks, but donated skin can sometimes cause infection, or the body may reject it. There are 2 million serious burn victims in the United States each year. Of these, 15,000 need skin grafts. The U.S. Red Cross estimates that less than 20 percent of the skin needed for burn victims is available from the nation's tissue banks. Skin is taken from organ donors after they die, but it can cost as much as $1,000 for 30 square centimeters (4.5 square inches). In addition, the strips of skin must be pieced together like a patchwork quilt. Donated skin may also be infected with viruses, including HIV. Using artificial skin can help to solve these problems.

The process of making artificial skin starts with a soupy mixture of skin cells that is pumped onto an ultrathin plastic mesh. Within a week the cells multiply and fill the mesh to produce a layer of skin. This is then frozen until it is needed. A surgeon then thaws the patch and stretches it over a burn, leaving it there until the patient is ready for a graft. The artificial skin is only temporary, but it allows the patient's own skin to heal until it is ready for a skin graft. In the future it may be possible to develop a permanent skin, which would mean that skin grafts would no longer be needed.

Organs for Transplants

Many patients who need organ transplants soon discover there is a shortage of donor organs. There are far more people on waiting lists to receive a transplant than there are donors. Many patients suffer long periods of illness or even die while waiting for an organ. When organs are available, there are problems with transplantation. The major problem is rejection. The body of a patient may identify a transplant as being foreign and start to attack it.

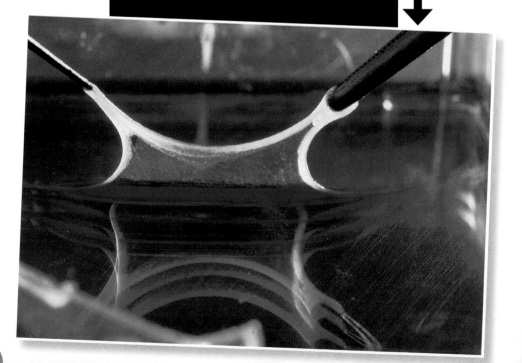

A layer of new skin cells is carefully removed from a culture solution. It can be used to treat the skin of people who have suffered from severe burns.

This heart is ready to be placed into the chest of a transplant patient. However, the patient will have to receive immunosuppressant drugs to stop rejection.

The human body's **immune system** is designed to attack anything it considers foreign in order to protect the body from disease. Unfortunately, the body cannot tell the difference between unwanted foreign bodies and desirable ones, such as a transplanted organ. Normally, a transplant patient is treated with immunosuppressant drugs, which stop the immune system from attacking the organ. However, this leaves patients less resistant to disease. In addition, the patient has to take the drugs for life to stop any rejection. Some patients, despite receiving the drugs, still reject a new organ.

Cloning could help transplant patients in three possible ways:
• by breeding animals especially for organs
• by building hearts, kidneys, livers, and other organs in a laboratory
• by using **stem cells**.

XENOTRANSPLANTATION

Animals could be used as a source of organs. The process of using an animal organ for transplanting into a human is known as xenotransplantation. The organs of pigs are the most compatible with humans and are easy to raise. However, the proteins on the surface of a pig's organs are very different from our own, so a human body would normally recognize them as being foreign and reject them. One solution is to genetically engineer a pig so that its organs would not be rejected when transplanted into a human. Scientists have identified a particular signal on the cells of human organs that, if present on pig cells, would prevent rejection. The gene that makes this protein has been identified and inserted into the DNA of a pig. The pig has been bred and there is now a small herd of pigs available for xenotransplantation in scientific trials in primates such as baboons. Unfortunately, pigs carry a number of viruses that could affect the human body, and scientists believe it is unlikely that it will be possible to breed virus-free pigs.

DISCUSS Xenotransplantation Issues

The raising of genetically engineered pigs purely for organ donation presents many issues. First, is it right to alter an animal in such a way that it can be used for organ transplantation? It could be argued that we raise animals for many purposes already, including food and leather. Pigs altered for the purposes of organ donation would have to be taken care of, kept in clean housing, and be well fed in order to ensure that the organs were of top quality. But what about the actual use of an animal organ to replace a diseased one in a human body? Many people feel uncomfortable with this idea. However, suppose you have an incurable heart disease and your only chance of survival is to have your heart replaced with a healthy pig's heart. Would you agree to the transplant? Some people would strongly object for religious reasons or because they consider pigs to be unclean. Some people do not eat pork or food derived from pigs and would consider the use of a pig's organs to be an unacceptable medical option. What do you think?

Animals such as pigs could be bred specifically as organ donors. However, this possibility raises numerous ethical and moral problems.

BUILDING WHOLE ORGANS

The second approach to helping transplant patients through cloning by making artificial organs is still at the early stages of development. However, scientists have successfully grown tissues such as skin and cartilage. Patients have had healthy cartilage cells from damaged knee joints removed and grown in the laboratory, before being transplanted back into the knee. Scientists have plans to eventually grow hearts, livers, and kidneys, too (see page 49).

Stem Cells

Much current research is centered on a particular type of cell called a stem cell. Stem cells are specialized, but unlike other specialized cells in the body, they can divide to make more cells. In addition, they have the ability to create other specialized cell types as they multiply. Stem cells occur at all stages of development from the embryo to the adult, but their versatility and numbers decrease with age. An embryonic stem cell has the ability to produce any one of the 200 different specialized cell types in the body, but an adult stem cell can only make a few.

It is the stem cell's ability to create other cell types that is of interest to scientists. Tissues, such as skin, intestines, and blood, undergo continual cell replacement. As some cells die, others are produced to replace them. The stem cells in these tissues continually divide to provide the replacement cells. Other types of tissue have a few stem cells that are not active until the tissue is damaged. For example, if damage occurs to muscle tissue, the stem cells start to divide again to repair the damage. However, many tissues do not have any stem cells, so the specialized cells cannot be replaced if they are damaged. For example, a person is born with millions of nerve cells in the brain. Each day some of these cells die. They are not replaced.

Some patients already have been treated using specialized cells that have been grown from stem cells in a laboratory. This is called cell replacement therapy. Patients suffering from extensive burns, leukemia, or degenerative diseases—such as Parkinson's disease (which affects the brain), diabetes (which affects the pancreas), hepatitis (which affects the liver), rheumatoid arthritis (which affects joints)—may be able to benefit from cell replacement therapy. Damaged organs or tissues could be injected with healthy, normal cells. When given the correct signal, these cells could regenerate the tissue around them. They could even produce new cells to replace those that have been damaged or killed.

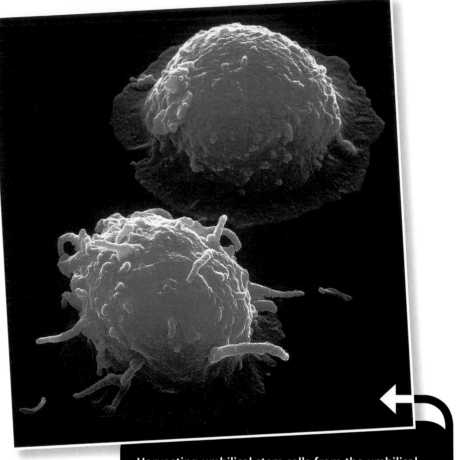

Harvesting umbilical stem cells from the umbilical cord of a baby raises fewer ethical objections than using cells from a developing embryo.

EMBRYONIC STEM CELLS

The best stem cells to work on are those taken from embryos that are about one week old. An embryo at this stage in its development is about the size of the period at the end of this sentence. It is made up of about 100 cells. Scientists can take a few of these cells and grow them for many weeks, so that they multiply to make many more stem cells. Once there are enough cells present, they can be treated in such a way as to start the process of cell specialization.

Stem cells can be taken from adults, but are not as useful. They grow for only a short time and produce fewer types and numbers of cell.

PREVENTING REJECTION

If the cells produced from foreign stem cells were simply injected into the body, they would be rejected just like a transplanted organ. However, rejection can be avoided by cloning the cells. The ideal method of treatment would be to take some stem cells from the patient and grow them in a laboratory in order to produce a supply of specialized cells that could be placed back inside the patient's body. Since the cells came from the patient, they would not be rejected. However, as adults only have a few stem cells with limited potential, the alternative approach is nuclear replacement. In this method, an embryonic cell has its nucleus removed and replaced with a nucleus taken from a cell of the patient. The cloned cell would grow into stem cells that would form the specialized cells for transplant.

Cloning cells for the treatment of medical conditions is called **therapeutic cloning**. In most countries, this research is regulated by laws. In the United States, therapeutic cloning is legal, but six states have laws that clearly prohibit it. In the UK, only approved research laboratories can carry out cloning on human embryos, and the embryos must not be more than 14 days old.

Even if therapeutic cloning was to become feasible, It would be a very expensive treatment. Most patients would not be able to afford such treatments, and it would be restricted to a few who could afford the treatments offered by private clinics. The issues concerned with research on human embryos are explored fully in the next chapter.

FOCUS   Cloning Adult Cells

In 2001 the privately funded U.S. company Advanced Cell Technology (ACT) announced that it had moved a step closer to cloning a human embryo. Using the nuclear transfer technique, ACT inserted adult DNA into unfertilized human eggs from which the nuclei had been removed. Some eggs started behaving like new embryos and began to divide. The most successful "embryo," however, reached only the six-cell stage. ACT's goal was to create a source of stem cells that could be used for therapeutic (not reproductive) purposes, so the experiment was not entirely successful. No egg divided long enough to start producing stem cells. ACT's announcement created a strong response. Some people saw the news as offering new hope for medical cures. Others, who opposed any type of cloning of human cells, condemned the ACT's work.

HUMAN CLONING

Human cloning is at the heart of the cloning debate. It is probably the one area of cloning that people have the most concern about. When asked about human cloning, many people think of Frankenstein's monster or have visions of people emerging from vats where they have been grown—all the stuff of science-fiction books and movies. How far have the scientists come along the road to this vision of the future?

In this chapter we will look at the issues associated with human **reproductive cloning**. This is very different from the therapeutic cloning described in the previous chapter. Reproductive cloning would involve the creation of a second, genetically identical human being, using a nucleus from a living person. This would be done by replacing the nucleus of a human egg cell with the nucleus from an adult cell. The modified embryo would then be implanted in a woman's uterus, where it would develop into a new individual.

It is important to remember that, unlike therapeutic cloning methods, the methods discussed in this chapter are theoretical. As yet, human reproductive cloning is not allowed in any country. In fact, it has been banned in many places, including Britain and other European countries.

In Vitro Fertilization (IVF)

The first step on the road to human cloning started with the first test-tube baby in 1978. This made use of a revolutionary technique in which a human egg was fertilized outside the body. Today, this technique, called in vitro fertilization (IVF), is carried out routinely on **infertile** women.

Infertility is often caused by blocked fallopian tubes, which lead from a woman's ovaries (where her eggs are stored). Fertilization normally takes place in one of the fallopian tubes. IVF treatment involves removing some of the woman's eggs from her ovaries and fertilizing them externally. The resulting embryo is returned to her uterus so pregnancy can proceed as normal.

This is a newly fertilized egg (zygote). The yellow hairlike structures are sperm still attached to it. After in vitro fertilization, this cell is cultured in a laboratory until it has grown into a ball of eight cells. Then it is placed in the mother's uterus.

FOCUS Test-Tube Babies

The first stage in IVF treatment is hormone treatment to get a woman's ovaries to produce many eggs. The eggs are collected by inserting a hollow needle through the wall of the vagina (the passageway leading to the uterus). The eggs are placed in a fluid that is similar to the one that exists in the fallopian tubes. Healthy sperm are added to the fluid, and fertilization takes place. The fertilized egg cells are grown until they reach the four to eight-cell embryo stage. The embryos are examined to make sure they are healthy, and then two or three are implanted in the uterus. By implanting more than one, there is a greater chance of success. Occasionally, all three survive and the woman gives birth to triplets. Any unused embryos can be stored in **liquid nitrogen** in case the first attempt is unsuccessful. Sometimes, women may give permission for any spare embryos to be used for research.

Treating Infertility

A lot of research into human infertility is taking place. However, some people feel that even more could be done if doctors were allowed to use cloning techniques in the treatment of infertility. The UK took an early lead in the treatment of infertility and is a leader in stem-cell research. In 1991 Britain established the Human Fertilization and Embryology Authority, which controls the creation, use, and storage of human embryos outside the body. In Britain it is illegal to carry out research on a human embryo more than 14 days old. In the United States, a few states completely prohibit the use of embryos for research.

Infertility can be a very emotional topic. A lot of childless couples feel that their lives are incomplete without children. Some fertility clinics are pushing for the rules on human reproductive cloning to be relaxed so that they can treat infertile couples more successfully. In the future, it is possible that the rules will be relaxed to help infertile couples have children. This could mean that the cloning of early embryo cells will be allowed. The process mimics the natural process that results in identical twins.

Identical twins are formed when an early embryo splits into two to form two separate individuals.

Sometimes, an embryo splits in two and the two parts continue to develop normally, creating identical twins or even triplets. Doctors could recreate this in the laboratory. An embryo could be produced by IVF. Then the cells of the early embryo could be separated to make several identical embryos, or clones (this procedure is described on page 23). One embryo could then be implanted in a woman's uterus. The rest of the embryos could be frozen for future attempts. As a result, a woman could have identical twins or triplets, born several years apart.

DISCUSS Cloning Advantages and Other Concerns

IVF treatment is very painful for the woman and is not without risk. It would be safer and cheaper for a laboratory to take one egg, fertilize it, and then split it to create many embryos. These embryos could develop into individuals identical to one another, but different from their parents. As an alternative, a woman who could not produce healthy eggs or had stopped producing eggs could use eggs from a donor. The nucleus could be removed from the donor egg and replaced with DNA from either the mother or the father. This way, the child would be a clone of one of its parents.

There are other procedures that could help women who miscarry. One of the causes of a **miscarriage** is faulty **cytoplasm** in the cells of an embryo. This could be overcome by using a cloning technique. First, a fertilized egg cell could be produced using IVF. The nucleus of this cell could be removed and placed inside an empty donor egg with a healthy cytoplasm. The genetic material would come from the mother and the father, but would be present in a cell with healthy cytoplasm, so the woman would not miscarry.

Many people are not opposed to the process of embryo cloning, but they are very concerned about the welfare of the children that are born as a result of this process. Ian Wilmut, the creator of Dolly, was asked whether he was opposed to multiple embryos. He replied that he did not object to the process, but only if all the embryos were used at the same time, so the mother gave birth to identical twins or triplets. He did not like the idea of freezing surplus embryos for use at a future date. His fear was that a newborn baby could be a clone of an older child. The older child would have already developed his or her own identity. Because the younger child would have the same appearance, he or she might not be treated as a unique individual. What do you think? How would you feel if you were the younger child? Or if you were the older child seeing a younger version of yourself?

Is Cloning Safer than Reproduction?

Some scientists argue that cloning is safer than sexual reproduction. The fertilization process is not 100 percent perfect. One of the most common causes of human birth defects is having too few or too many chromosomes. The chances of a chromosome abnormality increase with age, especially in mothers over the age of 40. If there is a serious defect, an embryo does not survive. A few may survive for a short time, but die in the mother's womb, and then the mother suffers a miscarriage. However, a small percentage will be born.

The most common chromosome disorder is having one chromosome too many. For example, the condition known as Down syndrome is caused by the presence of an extra copy of one small chromosome. Chromosome disorders would not happen with cloning because only healthy cells with the correct number of chromosomes would be used. Some babies are born with genetic disorders, such as cystic fibrosis or sickle-cell anaemia. Cloning would prevent this, too, since the cloned cells would be screened to ensure they do not have any genetic defects.

If you look carefully at this photograph of chromosomes taken from a person with Down syndrome, you will see that there are 47 chromosomes, instead of 46. Normally, there are two copies of each chromosome. But this individual has three copies of chromosome number 21 (bottom row of chromosomes).

Donor Clones

Some people worry that clones could be produced for the sole purpose of using them as donors. The clone could be used as a donor in a number of ways. For example, parents who have a child suffering from a life-threatening illness, such as leukemia, might decide to clone the child in order to create an identical child who would be the perfect bone marrow donor. There is also the fear that clones could be created solely for the purpose of using them as a source of transplant organs. For example, a wealthy person with heart disease could pay to have a clone of himself or herself created, in order to use the clone's heart as a replacement. This possibility may sound strange, but there are people who would pay large sums of money to increase their own lifespan. Society must carefully consider the ethical issues that will probably lead to additional laws being made to regulate human cloning.

Is Human Cloning Realistic?

There are many practical reasons why human cloning is not carried out at the moment. During the research that went into creating Dolly, more than 400 unfertilized eggs were taken from donor ewes. Human IVF clinics obtain an average of five to 10 eggs at a time from each woman donor. This means that any clinic wanting to work in human cloning would need to recruit at least 40 volunteers for each prospective pregnancy. The actual number of eggs needed would be much greater than this, since there is less than a one-in-five chance of becoming pregnant following IVF. These figures suggest that the chances of establishing a successful pregnancy from a cloned human embryo are between three and 10 times lower than in sheep. During the experiments to produce Dolly, hundreds of embryos died. The same would probably happen with human embryos.

Who Would Do the Cloning?

Although human cloning is banned in most countries of the world, there is a strong possibility that somebody somewhere could carry it out. The most likely place for this to happen is a fertility clinic. Fertility clinics have doctors with expertise in removing eggs from women, carrying out in vitro fertilization, and embedding embryos in the uterus. This kind of expertise is not found in biotechnology companies or research laboratories.

Risks of Cloning

Many clones have abnormalities that cause them to die during pregnancy or soon after being born. Until these problems are overcome, most scientists believe that it is not right for anyone to carry out experiments on humans that could result in a malformed child.

Even if a cloned baby appeared to be normal, he or she could have hidden abnormalities. When adult cells are used to create a clone, mutations (changes in genetic material) can be transferred with them. For example, the resulting clone could have a shortened lifespan, an increased chance of cancer later in life, or one of thousands of other defects. Experience with cloning in farm animals may identify ways of reducing risk, but this is likely to take years.

The Debate About Human Embryo Research

The issue of human embryo research is surrounded by controversy. It continues to be debated by scientists and nonscientists and by governments. People who support therapeutic cloning research argue that the embryos that would be used for the research were produced by artificial fertilization in a laboratory. They maintain that the embryo is just a ball of cells that could not survive outside a mother's body.

Other people, especially those who are against **abortion**, believe that all embryos have the potential to develop into a new individual and do not approve of any form of human embryo research. They say that by destroying the embryos, researchers are killing a potential individual. They are also concerned that this research brings human cloning one step closer.

Many countries have placed at least a temporary ban on research using human embryos until the matter can be thoroughly debated. What would happen if the ban became permanent? Most importantly, it would stop research into potentially lifesaving medical procedures, such as the growing of organs for transplants. Would people want to give up this possibility? This is one of the key issues to be carefully considered by society and governments when deciding what kind of legislation should be passed regarding cloning research.

This embryo is at the eight-cell stage and the cells are identical and undifferentiated.

FOCUS Why 14 Days?

Research on embryos is only permitted for up to 14 days following fertilization. Up until 14 days, the embryo consists of a collection of dividing cells that are loosely clustered together. None of the cells has started to specialize. At 14 days, a change takes place and a groove appears on the upper side of the embryo. This is called the primitive streak. This marks the stage where the cells start to specialize. At this point, any experimentation has to stop and the embryos have to be destroyed.

Where to Draw the Line?

The difficulty lies in deciding where to draw the line. When does research into lifesaving medical procedures stop and creating a baby that is a clone start? What about childless couples who are desperate for a baby? Is it okay to allow research into infertility? Would it be okay to clone a human from a cell taken from an early embryo rather than from a cell of a living adult? If you were dying from heart disease would you want the opportunity to clone your heart for your own survival?

Answering these questions is difficult. Some people argue that if we really want to stop the possibility of human cloning we must stop all research, regardless of the benefits to human health. They fear that any research related to cloning would form the first few steps toward human clones.

In the United States, some lawmakers are pushing for legislation that would ban all human cloning. Should this happen, researchers in the United States, working for either privately or publicly funded companies, would not be allowed to carry out research on embryos for any purpose, including therapeutic reasons. Lawmakers in favor of such a law would call for heavy fines and a possible jail sentence for anyone who was discovered breaking the law.

In the UK, the government has decided to allow further research into human embryos to take place. After considering all the evidence, the government decided that the benefits from this type of research outweighed the risks. The British government, in an effort to calm worries that someone might try to clone a human, has also passed an act that specifically outlaws human cloning for reproductive purposes.

"The human embryo has a special status and we owe a measure of respect to the embryo. We also owe a measure of respect to the millions of people living with these devastating illnesses."

Lord Hunt, junior health minister, discussing the new law concerning research into human embryos in the UK, 2000

"I don't think there's any way that you can prevent the creation of human clones without stopping it from the very beginning. We're talking about crossing a threshold here. We're no longer talking about using the quote-unquote excess embryos in the freezers for stem cell research. We're now talking about creating embryos for destructive research purposes."

Representative Dave Weldon of Florida, who sponsored a bill in the House of Representatives that would ban human cloning

In 1995 John Habgood, former archbishop of York, cautioned against using genetic engineering to improve people. He gave six rules that he believed society should follow: "First, human beings are more than their genes. Genes are only a set of instructions. We are more than a set of instructions. Second rule: remember the valuable diversity of human nature. Third rule: look for justice in the dealings of human beings with one another and for fairness in the use of resources. Fourth rule: respect privacy and autonomy. Fifth rule: accept the presumption that diseases should be cured when it is possible to do so. And sixth rule: be very suspicious about improving human nature; and be even more suspicious of those who think they know what improvements ought to be made."

A Right to an Identity

One of the key issues with human cloning is the rights of cloned individuals to lead their own lives and have their own genetic identity. This issue raises many questions: What sort of life would a cloned baby have? Would the child be owned by the clinic? If a famous person were to be cloned, would people expect the child to grow up to be exactly like that famous person? The same problem would exist for a child who was a clone of his or her parent. The child would look like the father or the mother, but would he or she be treated as an individual in his or her own right? There is no guarantee that a clone would have the same personality as the original individual.

Although clones are genetically identical, studies have shown that a person's personality and intelligence are affected by their environment. A clone many years younger than the original would be living in a different time, in different surroundings, eating different food, and having a different education. All these factors would affect their personality development. Although clones would look identical, they would probably behave differently. Laws would need to be written to protect the rights of these individuals and to prevent their exploitation. However, the laws would have to be flexible enough to accommodate future scientific developments.

FUTURE DEVELOPMENTS

In the movie *Jurassic Park*, a group of scientists recreated dinosaurs. They supposedly had found dinosaur DNA in the bodies of blood-sucking insects that had been preserved in amber (the hardened sap of a tree). They took this DNA, repaired it, replaced the missing parts with DNA from reptiles, and inserted it into an empty frog's egg. In the real world, there have been proposals to resurrect extinct animals, such as the dodo (a large, flightless bird) and the quagga (related to the zebra), using DNA from preserved specimens. The same idea has even been suggested in order to recreate famous dead people, including Elvis Presley! Despite the advances in gene technology and cloning, these kinds of possibilities are still some way off and may never occur.

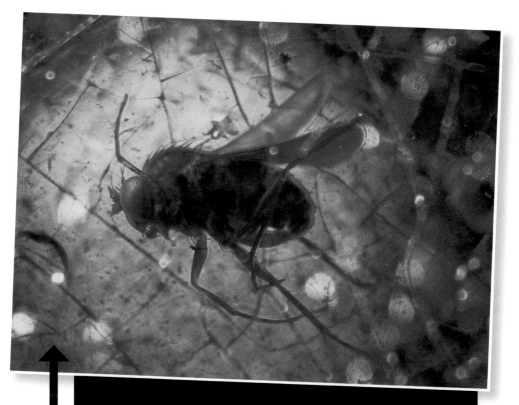

An insect that is millions of years old is preserved in amber. There is a theoretical possibility that the gut of a biting insect such as a mosquito, preserved in amber, could contain a tiny amount of blood taken from an animal, such as a dinosaur.

Growing Hearts, Livers, and Kidneys

In 1997 Dr. Charles Vacanti of the University of Massachusetts implanted an ear-shaped mold made of biodegradable plastic onto the back of a mouse. The mouse had been genetically engineered not to reject human cells. Living, human cartilage cells were scattered over the mold. The cells grew and took on the shape of a human ear. Eventually, the plastic mold broke down, leaving just the living cells. The ear was then removed, without killing the mouse.

Some years from now, scientists may be growing whole hearts, livers, and even arms and legs in high-tech labs. Organs will probably be grown in parts. For example, a heart may be built as valves, muscle, and blood vessels that would be joined together to form a heart. One patient could have just his or her faulty heart valves replaced, while another might have the whole heart replaced.

FOCUS   Growing a Dog's Bladder

Researchers have already successfully grown artificial bladders for dogs, using tissue taken from normal dogs' bladders. Scientists grew the cells in a lab so there were plenty to use to make the new organ. Then they made a 3-D support structure in the shape of the bladder. This was "seeded" with bladder cells covered in specially formulated solutions. The cells started to grow and spread along the support structure until they reached the end before they stopped growing. Once the tissue was in place, the support structure was designed to break down and disappear. The bladder took six weeks to grow. It was then transplanted into a dog. It functioned in the dog for 11 months. Then, in 2006, a similar procedure was carried out successfully on seven human patients. Similar techniques could be used to build hearts, livers, and kidneys. However, these organs are more complex than a bladder and would probably take several months to grow. The problems encountered by the scientists included making sure there was enough oxygen and nutrients and ensuring the structure allowed the cells to grow into the right shape.

It may be possible to grow a whole new arm or leg for a patient who has suffered an amputation. A whole limb offers a major challenge, however, since it is made up of many cell types that form different tissues. The support structure would have to be seeded with different cells and these cells would have to be encouraged to grow together.

Saving Rare Animals

More animals than ever before are now listed as being endangered. This often happens as a result of the introduction of new species that compete for limited resources, the loss of natural habitat, or hunting. Some species are on the brink of extinction. Spix's macaw and a sole surviving individual of a giant tortoise subspecies found on the Galapagos Islands are two examples of nearly extinct species. Some of these animals are old and unable to breed, so new individuals are unlikely to be born.

The Galapagos giant tortoise is an endangered species of reptile. The number of these tortoises is dangerously low, and many of the animals are very old.

Wild animals are not the only ones under threat. Many indigenous breeds of livestock (those that orginate naturally in a region) are under threat from imported breeds that humans have introduced. The local breeds may have valuable genes that help them to survive in hot conditions or that give them resistance to disease. There is therefore an urgent need to prevent their extinction. Current conservation methods involve the storage of frozen semen or embryos, but this is time-consuming and costly. As a result, only a few of the threatened species are being protected in this way. Cloning may provide another option.

FOCUS Animal Cloning Experiments

Experiments have already taken place with gaurs—endangered wild oxen found in India. A research team took 692 skin cells from a dead gaur and fused them with cows' eggs that had their nuclei removed. Of these, 40 developed into embryos and were placed in surrogate cows. Eight of the cows became pregnant, and one calf was born. He was named Noah. Noah died shortly after birth from a bacterial infection that affects many newborn animals. An experiment planned for the future involves the *bucardo* (a mountain goat that lived in Spain). Unfortunately, the last surviving bucardo, a female, was killed by a falling tree. Tissue samples were taken, and she will be cloned. However, all the clones will be female. Chromosomes from the goat species that is most closely related to the bucardo will be needed to create a male mountain goat.

Endangered populations with only a few breeding individuals are at risk from inbreeding, that is, related animals breeding with each other. Inbreeding is a problem because it reduces genetic diversity. If a few individuals carry harmful genes, then there is a greater possibility that the genes will spread through the population. In a larger population, the genes would be "diluted" and have less of an effect on the health of the animals. Inbreeding tends to produce less-healthy animals that have a reduced resistance to disease. The same is true of cloning. All the individuals are the same, so there is no genetic diversity. The problem could be partly solved by taking cell samples from as many different individual animals as possible.

The gaur is an endangered species of wild ox that is found in India. Taking tissue samples from some of the remaining animals and storing them for future use could be one way to ensure the survival of this ox.

Frozen for the Future

Each cell of an animal's body—except the red blood cells—contains the full genetic code for the entire animal. Nuclear transfer provides a way of converting cells into whole animals. Cells from endangered breeds, collected from scrapings of the soft skin inside the mouth or from **hair follicles**, could be multiplied in a laboratory and frozen. The frozen cells could be stored indefinitely in liquid nitrogen. This is called cryopreservation. At some time in the future, a living population of animals could be reestablished from the frozen cells, using the same procedure that created Dolly.

DISCUSS   The Advantages of Cloning

Cloning has many advantages over the current methods of obtaining sperm and eggs. The collection of sperm and eggs from wild animals requires special skills and equipment. There is also an element of risk to the animal itself because it usually has to be sedated or even anesthetized. The number of embryos that are produced in this way is small, and there is a risk that none of the embryos will survive when they are eventually used. In contrast, collecting cells for cryopreservation would be relatively simple and could be done without special training. Also, cloning provides an unlimited supply of cells that could be used to keep trying for a successful pregnancy.

Cloning alone will not save rare species, but it is one way to save certain species until a better way is found and the reasons for the animals' decline are addressed. Do you think there is much point in cloning a whole new group of endangered animals if they have no habitat in which to live? For example, the giant panda eats bamboo, so it is found only in forests where there is bamboo. These forests are disappearing rapidly, and this is threatening the giant panda's survival. The cells of the giant panda could be frozen, but there would be no point in cloning giant pandas if there was nowhere for them to live. Similarly, some of the rarest macaws live in tropical rain forests. Not only are humans clearing the rain forest but they trap the macaws and sell them as pets. Would it be pointless to produce expensive clones of macaws for release back into the wild if they were to be illegally caught and sold by poachers? It could become necessary to keep the tissues of some endangered species in storage for several hundred years.

"If you produce lots of animals that are identical, you get inbreeding. They can't adapt to stresses, which is what evolution is about and why you need biological diversity."

Bill Holt of the Zoological Society of London, talking about the problems of a lack of diversity among clones of a single animal

"If I have to choose between extinction and cloning, I'll choose cloning every day."

Dr. Betsy Dresser of the Audubon Institute Center for Research of Endangered Species in New Orleans

Cloning and the "Frozen Zoo"

One of the leading centers for research into the cloning of endangered species is based at the Audubon Center in New Orleans. It has a collection of cells from more than 1,000 different species. This "frozen zoo" includes cells from the Sumatran tiger, mountain gorilla, and mountain bongo. It aims to save animals from extinction by storing cells for future research and possible cloning. So far, its most successful project has been the cloning of an African wildcat named Jazz, which it produced by inserting a wildcat embryo into the uterus of a domestic cat. Jazz was then cloned to make two more African wildcats.

"We're working through science to save species for the next generation. More and more zoos are involved. There are partnerships all over the world to save these species and put them back in their habitat."

Ron Forman, chief executive, Audubon Nature Institute

A technician removes a sample of bull semen that has been cryogenically preserved in liquid nitrogen, in a similar way to cells at the frozen zoo.

Designer Babies

Within the next 20 to 30 years, the technology will probably exist to enable people to design their own baby. By then scientists may know the position and sequence of every human gene and how they interact with one another. Already, doctors can take a cell from an unborn child and test the DNA for some genetic diseases. Techniques have been developed to genetically alter sperm cells in animals to ensure that specific characteristics are inherited in offspring. Soon, it will be possible to do this to human sperm. Initially, embryos produced by in vitro fertilization would be altered to eliminate unwanted genes, but there is the potential to do much more. People might decide that it would be acceptable to remove genes responsible for genetic diseases such as cystic fibrosis, muscular dystrophy, or hemophilia. But would it be acceptable to enhance traits such as creativity, fitness, or musical ability?

DISCUSS Enhancement: A Good Thing?

There is a genetically engineered strain of fruit fly that learns 10 times faster than normal flies. Imagine if humans had enhanced memories and learning abilities. People could learn more quickly and would not forget as much. This may sound appealing but many psychologists believe our ability to forget is very important—especially when it comes to unpleasant experiences. There is even some evidence to suggest that people who have total recall of events, or a photographic memory, are at a disadvantage. They can remember events that happened some time ago as clearly as if they happened yesterday. This can be very confusing.

There is, of course, a significant risk of people abusing the technology of cloning. In a world where money is important, it is possible that rich parents might demand that genetic engineering be used to "perfect" their unborn child. But who is to be the judge of what or who is perfect? And what would happen if something went wrong? Would the parents blame the doctor who carried out the alterations? Would people call for the technology to be banned?

The whole subject of human cloning and "designer babies" raises many ethical and moral questions. Many of the predictions seem far-fetched and are more like something you would see in a science fiction film. However, we must remember that there are many realities today that were just as difficult for people of previous generations to imagine.

CONCLUSION

When science presents something new, a common reaction is fear. The first baby produced by IVF, Louise Brown, was born in 1978. At the time, the IVF technique was extremely controversial. Today, IVF is common. During the 1970s, people were worried about recombinant DNA, which was the beginning of genetic engineering. There were even more worries when the first genetically modified (engineered) crops were grown. But these technologies are becoming part of our daily lives and so, one day, may cloning.

The arrival of Dolly focused the world's attention on the issues of cloning. Some people argue that these discussions should have been made before breakthroughs, such as the creation of Dolly, actually occurred. But it is impossible to predict all the potential developments of a technology. Developments such as the cloning of high-quality livestock will probably continue without much response from the public. Few people seem to object to the use of cloning in the conservation of endangered animals, but they may strongly object to recreating extinct ones.

Will a Ban Stop Fears?

The topics of human stem cell research and human reproductive cloning are generating great fear. Most governments have put a temporary ban on these fields of research. This has created a "breathing space" so that these controversial subjects can be carefully considered and discussed. However, there are many people who say it would be a mistake to rush to ban all research into human cloning. If research is completely banned, many of the benefits would be lost. History shows that however beneficial some technological developments can be to society as a whole, there will always be ways in which they can be misused. Many scientists believe that the solution is not to ban the technology itself, but to regulate it by passing laws that spell out exactly which procedures and techniques may be carried out and which may not.

Legislation Controls

Having balanced legislation in place is important. In many countries, licences are needed to carry out research on human embryos, and licence-holders are not allowed to place a cloned embryo into a uterus. Many nations have made or indicated that they will make human reproductive cloning illegal. Whatever happens, it is important that all the issues are carefully considered before making decisions that could affect the future of us all.

Looking Forward

Looking ahead, it seems likely that at some point in the future humans will be cloned, but it will probably not be called cloning. Cloning is a word that provokes emotional reactions, so it is likely that scientists may use another term, such as nuclear transfer. Meanwhile, society as a whole has time to think about which uses of cloning technology might be acceptable and which would not. What do you think?

> *"I think cloning is a good idea in certain situations—when a man has no sperm cells it could help him have a child. I am collaborating with colleagues outside Italy who are carrying out animal experiments. This sort of research is banned here, but there is no doubt that cloning will be a reality within a few years."*

Professor Antinori, the controversial Italian infertility specialist who has stated that he is ready to start cloning babies for infertile couples

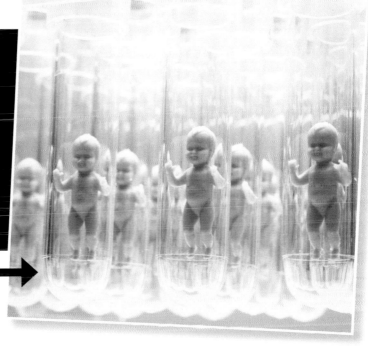

Could this be an accurate vision of the future? Will there ever be human clones? Scientists and other people will have to decide what is acceptable and what is not.

TIMELINE

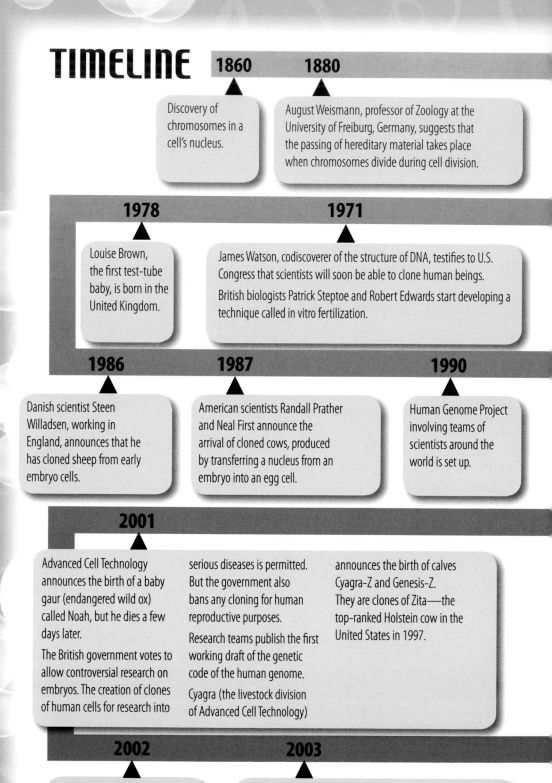

1860

Discovery of chromosomes in a cell's nucleus.

1880

August Weismann, professor of Zoology at the University of Freiburg, Germany, suggests that the passing of hereditary material takes place when chromosomes divide during cell division.

1978

Louise Brown, the first test-tube baby, is born in the United Kingdom.

1971

James Watson, codiscoverer of the structure of DNA, testifies to U.S. Congress that scientists will soon be able to clone human beings.

British biologists Patrick Steptoe and Robert Edwards start developing a technique called in vitro fertilization.

1986

Danish scientist Steen Willadsen, working in England, announces that he has cloned sheep from early embryo cells.

1987

American scientists Randall Prather and Neal First announce the arrival of cloned cows, produced by transferring a nucleus from an embryo into an egg cell.

1990

Human Genome Project involving teams of scientists around the world is set up.

2001

Advanced Cell Technology announces the birth of a baby gaur (endangered wild ox) called Noah, but he dies a few days later.

The British government votes to allow controversial research on embryos. The creation of clones of human cells for research into serious diseases is permitted. But the government also bans any cloning for human reproductive purposes.

Research teams publish the first working draft of the genetic code of the human genome.

Cyagra (the livestock division of Advanced Cell Technology) announces the birth of calves Cyagra-Z and Genesis-Z. They are clones of Zita—the top-ranked Holstein cow in the United States in 1997.

2002

California is the first U.S. state to legalize therapeutic cloning.

2003

The world's first cloned horse, Prometea, is born in Italy and is the genetic twin of her mother.

Dolly the sheep dies from lung disease, aged six.

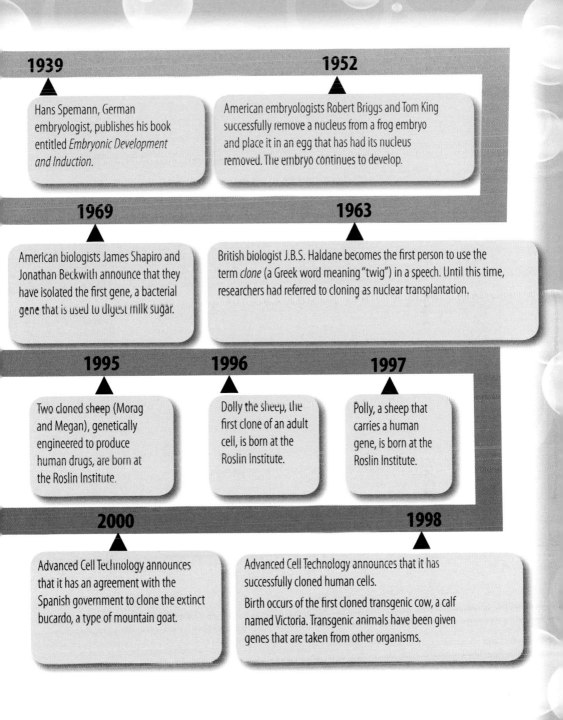

1939

Hans Spemann, German embryologist, publishes his book entitled *Embryonic Development and Induction*.

1952

American embryologists Robert Briggs and Tom King successfully remove a nucleus from a frog embryo and place it in an egg that has had its nucleus removed. The embryo continues to develop.

1969

American biologists James Shapiro and Jonathan Beckwith announce that they have isolated the first gene, a bacterial gene that is used to digest milk sugar.

1963

British biologist J.B.S. Haldane becomes the first person to use the term *clone* (a Greek word meaning "twig") in a speech. Until this time, researchers had referred to cloning as nuclear transplantation.

1995

Two cloned sheep (Morag and Megan), genetically engineered to produce human drugs, are born at the Roslin Institute.

1996

Dolly the sheep, the first clone of an adult cell, is born at the Roslin Institute.

1997

Polly, a sheep that carries a human gene, is born at the Roslin Institute.

2000

Advanced Cell Technology announces that it has an agreement with the Spanish government to clone the extinct bucardo, a type of mountain goat.

1998

Advanced Cell Technology announces that it has successfully cloned human cells.

Birth occurs of the first cloned transgenic cow, a calf named Victoria. Transgenic animals have been given genes that are taken from other organisms.

2005

Researchers at the University of Newcastle clone the first human embryo. The first cloned dog, an Afghan hound called Snuppy, is born in South Korea.

2008

U.S. Food and Drug Administration rules that milk and meat from cloned animals is safe to eat.

GLOSSARY

abortion termination of pregnancy

antibody special protein made by the immune system that attaches to any foreign cells and inactivates them

artificial insemination transfer of sperm from a male to a female in order to fertilize an egg without sexual intercourse

bone marrow liquidlike tissue found in the center of the body's largest bones, which produces red blood cells, white blood cells, and platelets

cellulose carbohydrate that forms a wall around plant cells

chromosome a threadlike structure in a nucleus, made up of DNA and protein

cytoplasm jellylike substance that fills a cell and in which the components of a cell are suspended

DNA (deoxyribonucleic acid) molecule that carries a genetic code, found in the nucleus of a cell

donor someone who donates an organ or body product, for example, bone marrow, to help someone who has a faulty organ or body product

embryo term for an egg after it has been fertilized, when it is in its early stages of development

embryology the study of embryos

encryption conversion of data into a code so that it cannot be read or accessed by an unauthorized person

endangered term for a species that is at risk of becoming extinct, or dying out

enzyme type of protein produced by living cells that is able to catalyze (increase the speed of) reactions within organisms

ethical to do with what is morally right or wrong

fertilization joining together of a male and female sex cell to form a new individual

gene unit of inheritance that is passed on from parent to offspring, made up of a length of DNA on a chromosome

genetic code sequence of chemical bases in DNA that codes for specific amino acids

genetic engineering (also called genetic modification) production of new combinations of genetic material through altering the DNA of an organism. Usually a gene from one organism is introduced into the DNA of another.

genetics the study of heredity, how different characteristics are inherited

growth medium solution (containing nutrients) on which organisms, such as bacteria, are grown

hair follicle small group of cells that surround and feed a hair

HIV (human immunodeficiency virus) virus responsible for AIDS (acquired immune deficiency syndrome). HIV is transmitted through the exchange of bodily fluids, primarily semen, blood, and blood products.

immune system system in the body that recognizes foreign cells and destroys them

infertile unable to produce offspring

in vitro fertilization (IVF) medical process in which an egg from a woman is fertilized in a glass Petri dish (*in vitro* means "in glass") in a laboratory. The embryo is then implanted in her uterus.

leukaemia cancer that affects white blood cells

liquid nitrogen nitrogen in a liquid state used to preserve cells at very low temperatures of about -196 °C (-320 °F)

miscarriage when a woman loses her baby during pregnancy

molecule smallest unit a chemical substance can be divided into while still having the properties of that substance

nuclear transfer transferring of a nucleus from one cell and placing it in an empty egg cell. The egg cell is then stimulated into dividing to produce an embryo.

nucleus central part of a cell that controls many cell functions and contains DNA

Parkinson's progressive disease of the nervous system, in which sufferers have difficulty controlling their muscle movements

photosynthesis process in which plants manufacture sugars and starch using carbon dioxide and water, in the presence of light. The process takes place in the chloroplasts, which contain a green pigment called chlorophyll.

protein large molecule made from amino acids, important for growth and repair. Found in foods including meat, dairy products, eggs, and fish.

recombinant DNA DNA that has been stitched together using DNA from different sources, for example, by inserting human gene DNA into the DNA of a bacterium

reproductive cloning the cloning cells to produce embryos that would develop into a new individual

semen mixture of sperm and fluids produced by male mammals when they ejaculate (discharge semen)

sexual reproduction fusion of gametes (egg and sperm) to create an offspring

sperm male sex cell

stem cell cell that retains the ability to divide and multiply and to create other types of cell. Stem cells are found in embryos, bone marrow, skin, intestine, and muscle tissue.

surrogate female animal that gives birth to another female's baby

therapeutic cloning cloning cells for the treatment of medical conditions and diseases

transplant to replace diseased tissue or organs with healthy tissue or organs from a donor

uterus organ of the female reproductive system in which the fetus (unborn child) grows and develops; also known as the womb

zygote fertilized egg cell

FIND OUT MORE

Further Reading

Engdahl, Sylvia, ed. *Cloning*. Detroit: Greenhaven Press, 2006.

Fullick, Ann. *Science at the Edge: In Vitro Fertilization*. Chicago: Heinemann Library, 2009.

Morgan, Sally. *Chain Reactions: From Microscopes to Stem Cell Research: Discovering Regenerative Medicine.* Chicago: Heinemann Library, 2006.

Morgan, Sally. *Chain Reactions: From Sea Urchins to Dolly the Sheep: Discovering Cloning.* Chicago: Heinemann Library, 2006.

Wilmut, Ian and Roger Highfield. *After Dolly: The Uses and Misuses of Human Cloning.* New York: W.W. Norton and Company, 2006.

Websites

www.advancedcell.com
This is the website for the company that has produced a range of cloned animals, including Noah, the first clone of an endangered animal.

www.audubonInstitute.org/site/PageServer?pagename=Facility_Research_Center
This is the web page for the Audubon Center for Research of Endangered Species.

http://learn.genetics.utah.edu/units/cloning
This useful web page is full of factual information about cloning—what it is, how it is done, what are the risks, cloning myths, and much more.

www.newscientist.com/home.ns
Many articles on cloning can be found here.

www.roslin.ac.uk
This website is run by the institute where Dolly was created. You can find a lot of background information on cloning and genetic engineering here, plus useful links to other sites.

INDEX